Essential Oils and Aromatherapy for Beginners:

Weight Loss, Health, and Natural Healing

Wait! Before You Continue...Are You On A Diet? Do You Want To Lose A Few Pounds?

If you answered YES to both questions, you not alone. Almost everyone wants to lose 10, 20, 30 or 50 pounds. Unfortunately, most of us have no idea how to do it. Yes, dieting can work, but starving yourself just leads to frustration and failure.

If you've been searching for weight loss tips that really work – you've found the right place.

Right now, you can get full **FREE access to WEIGHT LOSS REPORT** packed full of weight loss secrets so you can easily and quickly create THE BODY of your dreams.

Read it to the end and see **"FREE BONUS REPORT"**, after the Author page.

Medical Disclaimer

 Although the author and publisher have made every effort to ensure that the information in this book was correct at press time, the author and publisher do not assume and hereby disclaim any liability to any party for any loss, damage, or injury caused by errors or omissions, whether such errors or omissions result from negligence, accident, or any other cause. This book is not intended as a substitute for the medical advice of physicians. The reader should regularly consult a physician in matters relating to his/her health and particularly with respect to any symptoms that may require diagnosis or medical attention.

Contents

Introduction to Aromatherapy

I want to thank you and congratulate you for downloading the book, “Essential Oils and Aromatherapy for Beginners: Weight Loss, Health, and Natural Healing.”

The idea of using plants and its parts to extract oil for the use of psychological and physical well-being has no definite origin. Several civilizations had a part in contributing to it. The ancient Egyptians were said to have invented the distillation machinery as a means to expel oils from natural plants such as cedar wood, cinnamon and clove, which were significant with their rituals.

The Chinese also played a role by introducing the custom of using saturated aromatic oils to enhance the mood.

The Greek civilization followed suit, developing oil, for the first time, from myrrh. The "father of medicine" Hippocrates claimed to have recommended aromatherapy for the well-being of an individual.

The nomenclature "aromatherapy" was first coined in 1937 when French chemist Rene-Maurice Gattefosse formulated the word after he was involved in a bad fire accident, and the powerful healing abilities of essential oils cured him. Immediately afterwards, World War II recognized aromatherapy as a form of alternative medicine and utilized its medical benefits.

Aromatherapy is useful in additional ways one can see. It can relax you, it can help you handle and remedy certain ailments, and it also has been confirmed to be helpful in the cases of mental illnesses such as dementia or depression.

Essential plant oils can work very well, depending on how they are applied as part of a cure. The purpose of this is that they have the ability to affect both the mental and as well as the physical functions of our bodies.

Thanks again for downloading this book, I hope you enjoy it!

CHAPTER 1: Oil Profiles

Argan Oil:

Nicknamed as Morocco's liquid gold, this extract is derived from the little, oval nut of the rare Argan tree which is native to Morocco. The nut itself is protected by a dense peel which surrounds the succulent pulp, which in turn envelopes the highly sought after nut. Argan oil is widely used in its native country as a culinary ingredient, and since been claimed to be nutritious, chemo-preventive and anti-inflammatory.

The production and extraction of this essential oil is very unique. The fruit itself is air dried in the open and the fleshy pulp is removed. Some producers use machinery to discard the fleshy pulp, but no technology can be used to crack the nut which provides the oil, so this task is time consuming and requires magnificent effort from the Berber women, the people with the immense knowledge about Argan oil extraction.

When the oil is used for culinary purposes, the nut is slightly toasted, which gives the resulting oil a decadent nutty scent. When the oil is extracted for cosmetic purposes, the nut is cleaned, and pressed till the oil in its purest form is expelled. The oil is then left to settle its solidified residue at the bottom of the vessel for two weeks till it is filtered and categorized on its clarity and purity.

Argan oil is steeped with Vitamin E, ferulic acid, polyphenols, flavonoids, carotenoids and antioxidants making it one of the most important in aromatherapy. It has been successful due to its moisturizing effect which nourishes and helps eradicating wrinkles and premature aging. The proteins in the oil render the skin's elasticity, and also modifying the secretion of sebum according to your respective skin type.

This liquid gold, true to its name, serves almost every purpose the commercial cosmetics propose:

- ✓ Smoothes wrinkles
- ✓ Rejuvenates limp hair
- ✓ Prevents and fades stretch marks
- ✓ Repairs brittle nails
- ✓ Restores elasticity of skin

- ✓ All natural moisturizer
- ✓ Treats acne, eczema and other skin related conditions

Store this essential oil sealed tight, away from direct sunlight and fluctuating temperatures.

Bergamot Oil:

The bergamot categorized with the orange family and got its name from the place it was initially grown – *Bergomont*, which is in northern Italy. The bergamot plant is a small tree, producing smooth oval-shaped leaves and small fruits that are very similar to oranges. In fact, the bergamot plant is exclusively cultivated for the peel of its fruit. The essential oil extracted from bergamot is prized for its soothing properties and aroma. This oil is expelled from the peel of mature bergamot fruits, which contain the rejuvenating scent by a procedure called the cold press.

Bergamot essential oil has a refreshing and calming effect and is extensively used for garnering poise and self-confidence. Also, this therapeutic essential oil is useful in enhancing one's disposition. The aroma is particularly sought after by the perfumers, due to its capacity to merge easily with a wide range of fragrances to prepare a scent that balance each other.

The oil's zesty fragrance chiefly works on the nervous system and has the ability to calm down as well as energize the nerves.

According to an estimate, bergamot essential oil is a vital element in about a third of all perfumes intended for men, while it is included in roughly half the perfumes for women. In fact, bergamot was an ingredient of the first Eau de Cologne that was crafted in Germany in the 17th century.

The general properties in Bergamot Essential Oil are:

- ✓ antibacterial,
- ✓ antiviral,
- ✓ antispasmodic,
- ✓ anticancer,
- ✓ anti-inflammatory,
- ✓ analgesic,
- ✓ refreshing, and
- ✓ remedial.

The best blends for Bergamot Essential Oil are:

- ✓ eucalyptus,
- ✓ chamomile,
- ✓ geranium,
- ✓ juniper,
- ✓ jasmine,
- ✓ lavender,
- ✓ lemon,
- ✓ patchouli,
- ✓ and ylang ylang.

Precaution:

It is important to exercise caution while using this oil. Always remember, this should never be used in high concentrations on the skin, as it may cause irritation.

Natural Healing with Bergamot Essential Oil

The uplifting or inspiring features of this essential oil helps long suffering individuals with:

- ✓ Acne
- ✓ Anorexia
- ✓ Anxiety
- ✓ Asthma
- ✓ Boils and carbuncles
- ✓ Cystitis
- ✓ Depression
- ✓ Eczema
- ✓ Flatulence
- ✓ Gall bladder
- ✓ Grief
- ✓ Herpes
- ✓ High Blood Pressure
- ✓ Indigestion
- ✓ Loss of appetite
- ✓ Oily and open pores
- ✓ PMS
- ✓ Psoriasis
- ✓ Sore throat

- ✓ Ulcers
- ✓ Urinary infections
- ✓ Vaginal itching

Cedarwood Oil:

Cedar, indigenous to Lebanon, western Syria, and south central Turkey, has been used by the indigenous people since time immemorial, for many purposes. Ancient Egyptians used the concentrate to preserve mummies. Buddhists in Tibet made use of Cedarwood oil as incense, and the Greeks and Romans regarded it as medicinal. The timber of Cedarwood trees are acknowledged to be self-preserving and do not rot easily. This wood is used for outdoor purposes devoid of any treatment for resilience. The oil present in the timber of Cedarwood accounts for the self-preserving ability of the wood.

The oil is steam distilled from the timbers and bark of this tree, which lends a woody, musky and balsamic aroma. Cedarwood is extensively used as a room fragrance or potpourris owing to its pleasant warm fragrance.

Cedarwood essential oil has several beneficial properties, although it is usually used for its soporific effect. Apart from being useful in stress and strain management, this oil also has antiseptic and antispasmodic properties, which are efficient in treating a number of ailments. This oil may be used topically on injuries to clean, as well as avoid infections, such as tetanus. When Cedarwood oil is utilized in an aromatherapy diffuser, the air has the capacity to lessen coughing and even the flu. People with allergies fall asleep quickly and rest more profoundly. This action of the oil is attributed to the sedative property of Cedarwood essential oil. This essential oil is a strong emmenagogue and, hence, favorable for women, meaning, it encourages the flow of blood in the pelvic region. Cedarwood essential oil is anti-sebhorroeic- an incredible property that is unavailable in most essential oils.

The general properties in Cedarwood Essential Oil are:

- ✓ antiseptic,
- ✓ harmonizing
- ✓ detoxifying,
- ✓ soporific,
- ✓ stimulant, and
- ✓ anti-sebhorroeic.

The best blends for Cedarwood Essential Oil are:

- ✓ Bergamot,
- ✓ Cypress,
- ✓ Jasmine,
- ✓ Juniper,
- ✓ Neroli, and
- ✓ Rosemary.

Precaution:

Using Cedarwood oil in high concentrations may end in irritations. If you plan to use this oil internally, it is crucial that you consult a physician before usage.

Natural Healing with Cedarwood Essential Oil

The uplifting or inspiring features of this essential oil helps long suffering individuals with:

- ✓ Acne,
- ✓ alopecia,
- ✓ anxiety,
- ✓ arthritis,
- ✓ blood purifier,
- ✓ bronchitis,
- ✓ catarrh,
- ✓ colds and flu,
- ✓ coughs,
- ✓ cystitis,
- ✓ dandruff,
- ✓ dermatitis,
- ✓ eczema,
- ✓ gonorrhea,
- ✓ gout,
- ✓ hysteria,
- ✓ inflamed kidneys,
- ✓ insect repellent,
- ✓ insomnia,
- ✓ irritable skin,
- ✓ laryngitis,
- ✓ leucorrhea (vaginal discharge),
- ✓ lymphatic congestion,
- ✓ oily skin,
- ✓ panic,

- ✓ premenstrual syndrome,
- ✓ psoriasis,
- ✓ seborrhea of scalp,
- ✓ shock,
- ✓ sore throat,
- ✓ stress,
- ✓ thrush,
- ✓ toothache, and
- ✓ urinary tract infections.

Chamomile Oil:

Chamomile belongs to the daisy family. It is also recognized as Hungarian chamomile and true chamomile. The plant is native to Asia and Europe and is used for numerous therapeutic purposes. The Saxons believed this plant as a holy herb. The essential oil extorted from chamomile has been used for more than 2000 years for treating conditions, such as anxiety and insomnia. Egyptians also used this essential oil to treat common cold and fever. The concentrated oil is acquired from the freshly dried up flowers of this plant. The scent is pleasing and fruity, described similar to apples, hence its name from the Greek term *chamaimelon*, roughly meaning 'apple on the ground'. This essential oil is mild and has been usually utilized by herbalists for its ability to unwind the stressed nerves - mainly in the case of children, who are overactive or overexcited. Chamomile is also efficient for treating skin conditions, mainly soothing irritated skin. It is very relaxing bath oil and a calming and delicate room freshener.

Chamomile essential oils are offered in two varieties - Roman chamomile oil and German chamomile oil. The German chamomile is expelled from *Matricaria recutita* and is also referred to as the 'blue chamomile.' The Roman chamomile is the sweet chamomile or garden chamomile, because of its sweet fragrance. Roman chamomile is obtained from *Anthemis nobilis*. Both of these plants- Roman and German chamomiles - are found locally in the milder areas of Asia, where the plants are claimed to have their origin. Today, the herb is being cultivated in North America, Europe, Egypt and Australia and is grown widely in these places.

The general properties of Chamomile Essential Oil are:

- ✓ soothing,
- ✓ antiseptic,
- ✓ anti-inflammatory,
- ✓ tonic,
- ✓ digestive, and
- ✓ sedative.

The best blends for Chamomile Essential Oil are:

- ✓ Bergamot,
- ✓ Clary sage,
- ✓ Geranium,
- ✓ Jasmine,
- ✓ Lavender,
- ✓ Patchouli,
- ✓ Rose, and
- ✓ Ylang ylang.

Precaution:

There is a real risk of miscarriage, and pregnant women should refrain from using this oil.

Natural Healing with Chamomile Essential Oil:

The uplifting or inspiring features of this essential oil helps long suffering individuals with:

- ✓ fever,
- ✓ digestive problems,
- ✓ colic,
- ✓ diarrhea,
- ✓ teething problems,
- ✓ premenstrual tension and other menstrual problems,
- ✓ cystitis,
- ✓ headaches and migraine,
- ✓ earache,
- ✓ rheumatism,
- ✓ acne,
- ✓ dry skin,
- ✓ eczema,
- ✓ inflamed skin,
- ✓ irritability,
- ✓ loss of appetite,
- ✓ menopause,
- ✓ mood swings,
- ✓ nausea and vomiting,
- ✓ neuralgia,
- ✓ oversensitivity,
- ✓ sprains and stiffness,

- ✓ stomach pains,
- ✓ aches and pains,
- ✓ colitis,
- ✓ boils and carbuncles,
- ✓ burns,
- ✓ dandruff,
- ✓ depression,
- ✓ dermatitis
- ✓ enuresis,
- ✓ fluid retention,
- ✓ gall bladder,
- ✓ gum infections,
- ✓ heartburn,
- ✓ high blood pressure,
- ✓ hysteria and panic,
- ✓ immune system,
- ✓ inflammation,
- ✓ insomnia,
- ✓ vaginal itching,
- ✓ kidney infections / stones,
- ✓ liver, and
- ✓ lymphatic congestion.

Clary Sage Oil:

Ancient Greeks and Romans revered clary sage in high regard due to the herb's euphoric and aphrodisiac (sexual stimulant) features. The Germans too held clary sage greatly as it has the capacity to boost the alcoholic nature of their Muscatel wines.

Clary sage is an herb that thrives in heights and in most parts of the world. This strongly aromatic plant gives equally aromatic oil that is ecstatic, and also helps general health. The essential oil is extracted from the clary sage's flowers and foliage.

Along with its therapeutic properties, this wonder herb graces the culinary world, mainly in soups and stews. The balmy essential oil dominates the industrial sectors by being one of the most demanded fragrances by the perfumers worldwide. The exciting and stirring nutty notes in the oil create a feeling of well-being and contentment. Eliminating anxiety and nervousness, this oil aids when one is going through changes in life and helps focus and concentration.

The general properties of Clary Sage Essential Oil are:

- ✓ Antiseptic,
- ✓ anti-spasmodic,
- ✓ anti-sudorific,
- ✓ blood cleansing,
- ✓ stimulant,
- ✓ tonic, and
- ✓ warming.

The best blends for Clary Sage Essential Oil are:

- ✓ Bergamot,
- ✓ Frankincense,
- ✓ Geranium,
- ✓ Jasmine,
- ✓ Juniper,
- ✓ Lavender, &
- ✓ Sandalwood.

Precaution

Never use this essential oil before driving or undertaking any work that needs prime focus, as this may cause dizziness.

Natural Healing with Clary Sage Essential Oil:

The uplifting or inspiring features of this essential oil helps long suffering individuals with:

- ✓ Abscesses,
- ✓ animal bites,
- ✓ asthma,
- ✓ boils,
- ✓ bruises,
- ✓ burns,

- ✓ catarrh,
- ✓ cuts,
- ✓ depression,
- ✓ eczema,
- ✓ fatigue,
- ✓ gum disease,
- ✓ hair loss,
- ✓ headaches,
- ✓ herpes,
- ✓ laryngitis,
- ✓ menopause,
- ✓ palpitations,
- ✓ painful menstruation,
- ✓ poor concentration,
- ✓ stress,
- ✓ sweating,
- ✓ tonsillitis,
- ✓ urinary tract infections.

Eucalyptus Oil:

Eucalyptus is indigenous to Australia, but is being cultivated across the globe today. The leaves of this tree are the only supply of food for the koala bear. Homes around the world have found that planting these trees in their gardens abolishes parasites and fleas, due to the strong antiseptic property that eucalyptus is known for.

The oil from the foliage of this lofty tree is carefully distilled. Eucalyptus oil is a very practical treatment to invigorate the body, strengthen the immune system and offer shield from cold during the wintry weather. This oil has a simple element that assists in soothing down stimulated feelings. Also, this oil has sanitization and harmonizing properties that make it important for topical use in areas that are affected by emotional or physical pain.

Eucalyptus essential oil has an exciting and invigorating scent and it may be utilized to help improve concentration and disposition. The essential oil the most common natural oils that can be discerned due to its aroma which resembles camphor. It is wise to always carry a cotton ball steeped in eucalyptus oil in an airtight bag. One may open the bag and inhale the aroma deeply during the day, as the energy and focus are at their lowest. Having the cotton ball throughout the cold and virus time of the year, guards you from the microbes breathed out by people. Hence, this essential oil is a necessity for any medicine cupboard.

The general properties of Eucalyptus Essential Oil are:

- ✓ anti-catarrhal,
- ✓ antiseptic,
- ✓ stimulant, &
- ✓ decongestant.

The best blends for Eucalyptus Essential Oil are:

- ✓ Bergamot,
- ✓ Juniper,
- ✓ Lavender,
- ✓ Lemon,&
- ✓ Rosemary.

Precaution

This potent essential oil has the ability to be fatal if used orally.

Expectant and lactating mothers should keep away from this strong oil.

Natural Healing with Eucalyptus Essential Oil:

The uplifting or inspiring features of this essential oil helps long suffering individuals with:

- ✓ arthritis,
- ✓ asthma,
- ✓ bronchitis,
- ✓ burns,
- ✓ catarrh,
- ✓ colds and flu,
- ✓ coughs,
- ✓ cuts,
- ✓ cystitis,
- ✓ diarrhea,
- ✓ emphysema,
- ✓ exhaustion,
- ✓ fever,
- ✓ fibroids,
- ✓ fluid retention,
- ✓ headaches,
- ✓ herpes,
- ✓ inflammation,
- ✓ kidney infection,
- ✓ kidney stones,

- ✓ laryngitis,
- ✓ measles,
- ✓ mood swings,
- ✓ muscular pain,
- ✓ nervous disorders,
- ✓ neuralgia,
- ✓ rheumatism,
- ✓ rhinitis,
- ✓ sinusitis,
- ✓ sprains and strains,
- ✓ stiffness,
- ✓ throat infections,
- ✓ tonsillitis, &
- ✓ urinary infections.

Jasmine Oil:

The Old French word Jasmine is originated from the Persian word '*yasmin'* signifying that this shrub is the "gift from God". Belonging to the olive family, this plant includes roughly 200 types of varieties around the world. The leaves may be evergreen or deciduous, depending on the locale. Jasmine is grown only for their sweet-smelling blossoms. The flowers are fragile and open only at sundown and are picked at daybreak during which the small petals are sealed closely. The petals typically stay fully bloomed between six and eight in the evenings when the heat lessens.

Jasmine essential oil is steam distilled which require immense amounts of flowers just to create one ounce of precious oil, which is understandably very expensive.

The very aromatic jasmines have been greatly cherished by diverse civilizations all over the world for centuries. An ancient Egyptian queen was so attracted by the perfume of jasmine that she adorned her hair frequently with it. In Indonesia, a genus of jasmine is the national flower which is extensively featured in a wedding ceremony. Pakistan's national flower is Jasmine officinal.

Jasmines are utilized in sacred rites in the Philippines, where people make garlands of jasmine ('sampaguita') to the Gods and Goddesses. Hindus revere jasmines as a holy flower offered to Lord Shiva and Lord Ganesha.

Authentic jasmine cannot be compared with the synthetic perfumes that are found in the shops.

The general properties of Jasmine Essential Oil are:

- ✓ Anti-depressant,
- ✓ aphrodisiac,
- ✓ soothing, &
- ✓ uplifting.
- ✓ The best blends for Jasmine Essential Oil are:
- ✓ Any essential oil but especially with:
- ✓ Bergamot,
- ✓ Clary Sage,
- ✓ Geranium,
- ✓ Rose,
- ✓ Sandalwood, &
- ✓ Ylang Ylang.

Precaution

The essential oil should by no means be utilized internally or consumed.

Natural Healing with Jasmine Essential Oil:

The uplifting or inspiring features of this essential oil helps long suffering individuals with:

- ✓ Anorexia,
- ✓ bulimia,
- ✓ apathy,
- ✓ childbirth,
- ✓ depression,
- ✓ dry sensitive skin,
- ✓ frigidity,
- ✓ impotence,
- ✓ breast milk production,
- ✓ lack of confidence,
- ✓ oversensitivity,&
- ✓ menopause.

Lavender Oil:

As one the most renowned essential oil providers, lavender, a member of the mint family, has been an important contributor to aromatherapy since time immemorial. The Romans bathed in water combined with lavender essential oil. In ancient Egypt, the Pharaohs applied this authentic essential oil as scent. England made use of lavender essential oil to include fragrance to their linen and as a successful insecticide.

It is assumed that this shrub is indigenous to Asia, but with time, it has been launched in numerous areas, including the Mediterranean, Africa, Arabia, India and Western Iran. Because lavender oil has the capacity to effortlessly blend with other essential oils, it has constantly been the favored organic oil with the perfumers and cosmeticians. Lavender flowers are in spirals and they are held up in barbs that ascend above the bushes. The flowers differ in shade - violet, blue or lilac. The oil of lavender is produced by gleaning the fragrant floral spikes of a number of lavender species and sometimes even the leaves and stems. This oil is greatly treasured by people for its versatile utility.

The general properties of Lavender Essential Oil are:

- ✓ anti-inflammatory,
- ✓ antiseptic,
- ✓ antispasmodic,
- ✓ balancing,
- ✓ carminative,
- ✓ circulatory,
- ✓ detoxifying,
- ✓ diuretic,
- ✓ relaxing,
- ✓ stimulant,
- ✓ stomachic,
- ✓ tonic,
- ✓ uplifting, &
- ✓ vulnerary.

The best blends for Lavender Essential Oil are:

- ✓ eucalyptus,
- ✓ geranium,
- ✓ jasmine,
- ✓ lemon,
- ✓ orange,
- ✓ rose, &
- ✓ ylang ylang.

Precaution

Patients enduring chemotherapeutic treatments for any type of cancer should refrain from this oil.

Natural Healing with Lavender Essential Oil

The uplifting or inspiring features of this essential oil helps long suffering individuals with:

✓ aging / mature skin,	✓ Headache,
✓ allergy,	✓ high blood pressure,
✓ anal fistula,	✓ hysteria and panic,
✓ anorexia,	✓ immune system,
✓ arthritis,	✓ inflammation,
✓ athlete's foot,	✓ insomnia,
✓ boils and carbuncles,	✓ liver,
✓ bronchitis,	✓ menopause,
✓ bruises,	✓ migraine,
✓ burns,	✓ mood swings,
✓ catarrh,	✓ motion sickness,
✓ chilblains,	✓ myalgic encephalomyelitis,
✓ childbirth,	✓ nausea and vomiting,
✓ circulatory problems,	✓ oily and open pores,
✓ colds and flu,	✓ oversensitivity,
✓ cold sores,	✓ pains,
✓ colic,	✓ palpitations,
✓ colitis,	✓ premenstrual tension and other, menstrual problems,
✓ coughs,	✓ psoriasis,
✓ cystitis,	✓ rejuvenation,
✓ depression,	✓ rheumatism,
✓ dermatitis,	✓ rhinitis,
✓ digestive disorders,	

✓ diarrhea, ✓ earache, ✓ enuresis, ✓ exhaustion, ✓ fainting and vertigo, ✓ fast breath, ✓ fever, ✓ fibroids, ✓ flatulence, ✓ fluid retention, ✓ glandular fever, ✓ hair loss,	✓ irritability, ✓ scabies, ✓ shortness of breath, ✓ sinusitis, ✓ sprains and strains, ✓ stiffness, ✓ stomach pains, ✓ sunburn, ✓ throat infection, ✓ tonsillitis, ✓ thrush, ✓ ulcers, ✓ urination (difficulty of), and ✓ whooping cough.

Lemon Oil:

Lemons, which are in the class of citrus, are original to Asia, but are grown all over the Mediterranean, mainly in Portugal and Spain, and including California today. The trees bloom all through the year, even though it is very sensitive to cold and heat. The fragrance of lemon is famous and is a much loved with most people worldwide, and even with the ancient Egyptians who applied lemon essential oil as a cure for food poisoning and to treat fever outbreaks, and even as a perfume.

The essential oil is lovingly nicknamed as the 'golden gift of the sun', as the bright peels of the fruit produce the oil which inspires energy and exuberance to the body, mind and soul. Europeans normally use this as a natural antiseptic, especially when in times of disease and ill health.

To make this valuable extract, the rind of the lemon is removed and soaked in boiling water to make it pliable. One of the procedures of extracting the oil is by positioning a sponge alongside the yellowish face of the peel and squeezing it until the sponge is entirely drenched with lemon essential oil.

The other process involves technology. The peels are collected and rolled in a machine filled with spikes. The spikes will break the oil cells in the rinds and the oils are collected in a basin.

The general properties of lemon Essential Oil are:

- ✓ antibacterial,
- ✓ antiviral,
- ✓ carminative,
- ✓ digestive,
- ✓ diuretic,
- ✓ fungicidal,
- ✓ stimulant,
- ✓ stomachic,
- ✓ tonic, &
- ✓ enriching.

The best blends for Lemon Essential Oil are:

- ✓ eucalyptus,
- ✓ frankincense,
- ✓ geranium,
- ✓ juniper,
- ✓ lavender,
- ✓ roman chamomile,
- ✓ rose,
- ✓ sandalwood, &
- ✓ ylang ylang.

Precaution

Lemon essential oil has a very short shelf life and does not keep well for a long time.

Natural Healing with Lemon Essential Oil:

The uplifting or inspiring features of this essential oil helps long suffering individuals with:

- ✓ Acne,
- ✓ aches,
- ✓ anemia,
- ✓ arthritis,

- ✓ bronchitis,
- ✓ catarrh,
- ✓ chilblains,
- ✓ colds,
- ✓ coughs and flu,
- ✓ cuts,
- ✓ fluid retention,
- ✓ gout,
- ✓ gum infections,
- ✓ high blood pressure,
- ✓ hyperacidity of stomach,
- ✓ kidney infections / stones,
- ✓ mouth and tongue inflammations and ulcers,
- ✓ neuralgia,
- ✓ oily and open pores,
- ✓ pains,
- ✓ poor circulation,
- ✓ premenstrual tension,
- ✓ rheumatism,
- ✓ scabies, &
- ✓ varicose veins.

Peppermint Oil:

Peppermint is a fusion between the spearmint and watermint. The herb is indigenous to Europe, but today, it is found in almost all homes worldwide. This everlasting herb has many therapeutic aptitudes that were utilized extensively by the Indians, Egyptians and Chinese for several centuries. Ancient Romans used to make peppermint crowns and wear them during celebrations. Its intense and fiery scent has made peppermint a favorite among people since it revitalizes the body and mind.

The general properties of Peppermint Essential Oil are:

- ✓ Anti-bacterial,
- ✓ antispasmodic,
- ✓ carminative,
- ✓ stimulant,
- ✓ stomachic, &
- ✓ tonic.

The best blends for Peppermint Essential Oil are:

- ✓ Eucalyptus,
- ✓ juniper,
- ✓ lemon,
- ✓ rosemary,
- ✓ rosewood.

Precaution

This essential oil should be used with great restraint, as one undiluted drop can be very dangerous for children and adults with sensitive skin.

Natural Healing with Peppermint Essential Oil

The uplifting or inspiring features of this essential oil helps long suffering individuals with:

- ✓ Abdominal pains,
- ✓ acne,
- ✓ anorexia nervosa,
- ✓ bites,
- ✓ bruises,
- ✓ colic,
- ✓ coughing,
- ✓ mouth thrush,
- ✓ mouth ulcers,
- ✓ nausea,
- ✓ painful menstruation,
- ✓ stings,
- ✓ stress,
- ✓ swollen gums, &
- ✓ toothache.

Sandalwood Oil:

When it comes to sandalwood, the trees grown in Mysore, India are the best, because they produce the best quality oil in the world. Countries like Australia and Hawaii also have their own genus of sandalwood but none come closer to their Indian counterpart, as they do not give quality oil. The price of Indian sandalwood is extremely costly and on the brink of being extinct. For the Hindus, sandalwood is a crucial product in every occasion from birth to death. It is also considered holy and is given great respect.

Sandalwood essential oil is extracted from little pieces of timber from matured sandalwood trees by steam distillation. Wood from the trees which are of 80 years of age should be used for this process. Nevertheless, bearing in mind the scarcity of this genus, the oil is extracted from trees that are between 40 years and 80 years old. The fairly older sandalwood trees will not only yield more quantities of the essential oil, but its fragrance too would be more strong or rich. Original sandalwood oil is heavy and has a luxurious golden hue.

The general properties of Sandalwood Essential Oil are:

- ✓ Anti-inflammatory,
- ✓ antispasmodic,
- ✓ aphrodisiac,
- ✓ astringent,
- ✓ diuretic,
- ✓ comforting, &
- ✓ tonic.

The best blends for Sandalwood Essential Oil are:

- ✓ Bergamot,
- ✓ frankincense,
- ✓ geranium,
- ✓ jasmine,

- ✓ lavender,
- ✓ lemon,
- ✓ rose, &
- ✓ ylang ylang.

Precaution

The essential oil is not only very expensive, but also a rare product.

Natural Healing with Sandalwood Essential Oil

The uplifting or inspiring features of this essential oil helps long suffering individuals with:

- ✓ Abscesses,
- ✓ acne,
- ✓ anorexia,
- ✓ anxiety,
- ✓ broken capillaries,
- ✓ catarrh,
- ✓ coughs and colds,
- ✓ cystitis,
- ✓ depression,
- ✓ diarrhea,
- ✓ dry and chapped skin,
- ✓ eczema,

- ✓ fearfulness,
- ✓ fluid retention,
- ✓ frigidity,
- ✓ impotence,
- ✓ insomnia,
- ✓ laryngitis,
- ✓ menopause, &
- ✓ urinary infections.

CHAPTER 2: Essential Oils and Weight Loss

How can aromatherapy help us shed those nasty pounds?

Dropping weight is more than merely calories in vs. calories out. There are mental aspects involved in craving, motivation, and eating for emotional reasons.

Our sense of smell helps us with management and resolution. People discover that some essential oils cut appetite and encourage feelings of fullness. This only succeeds in an arrangement with a wholesome diet and exercise schedule. It will not work on its own but it can make diet plans work.

- ✓ Grapefruit Oil
- ✓ Lemon Oil
- ✓ Peppermint Oil
- ✓ Fennel Oil
- ✓ Bergamot Oil
- ✓ Cinnamon Oil
- ✓ Ginger Oil

Grapefruit Oil

Grapefruit essential oil is a strong concentrate taken from the grapefruit peels, much like any citrus essential oils. Having been utilized for centuries to overcome soreness, weight gain, sugar cravings, and withdrawal symptoms, it is believed to be nature's stress-combatant, anti-inflammatory, and cancer prevention. It is valued by those trying to lose weight. It helps augment energy levels and endurance, also eradicating sugar cravings.

Grapefruit has several active ingredients that are favorable to improve metabolism and trim down your hunger pangs.

Mix several beads of grapefruit essential oil to your water, disperse the vapors using a diffuser in your workplace or home, or rub some onto your upper body and wrists when an urge for food hits.

Moreover, grapefruit can be very successful for getting rid of surplus water weight because it helps launch a more active lymphatic system.

Lemon Oil

This essential oil is known as well to boost metabolism, curb appetite and advance digestive health. It can be breathed in by adding a few droplets to a cotton ball and calmly breathing the vapors prior to a meal to cut cravings and stay away from overindulging.

It can also be consumed by mixing 1 – 2 drops of medical grade lemon oil to a glass of water to improve your metabolism during the day.

Peppermint Oil

This oil is celebrated for its aid in improving metabolism, calming a distressed abdomen and improving digestion. It gives a sense of fullness after a meal, increases energy levels and ends cravings. Peppermint essential oil can be inhaled, simply soak a cotton ball in a few drops of the essential oil and inhale the scent ahead of a meal. This will assist to restrain cravings with the intention that one does not overindulge; or peppermint oil can be administered in the form of a refreshing minty bath.

Fennel Oil

Fennel essential oil, steam distilled from fennel seeds, possesses an earthy yet pleasant fragrance. Fennel has the hormone that physically controls circadian rhythms by alerting the brain of its every day wake-sleep sequences.

Together with promoting a good rest, this hormone -melatonin- trims down weight by generating more fat that burns off the other fat.

Long ago, fennel seeds were consumed to curb the hunger during fasting. This initiative has acquired scientific claim through a fennel oil aromatherapy done on mice. The rodents were exposed to fennel oil two times a day for 10 minutes for eight weeks; this showed that smaller quantities of calories were eaten and digestion was swifter.

Bergamot Oil

As mentioned previously in the oil profile, the scent of bergamots is pleasing and inspiring. It is full of polyphenols, something only green tea has, which aids to enhance metabolism by burning sugar and fats. We turn to unwholesome junk food when we are under psychological distress. By using bergamot oil, a sense of calmness and fulfillment takes over the endocrine system.

It can be breathed in by sprinkling a few droplets on a cloth and slowly inhaling, when a passion for food appears.

Cinnamon Oil

Cinnamon oil also enhances metabolism and assists in curbing cravings by converting sugars to energy instead of fat. If it is to be consumed, mix two drops of medical grade cinnamon oil with a cup of lukewarm water with a tiny bit of honey and drink prior to meals.

Cinnamon oil can also be breathed in by soaking a cotton ball in its oil and slowly inhaling the vapors.

Ginger Oil

The ginger root possesses gingerol, a natural composite with potent anti-inflammatory effects. Gingerol amplifies thermogenesis, thus advancing metabolism. To consume ginger oil, it is recommended that one adds a drop or two to their black tea or fill it within a capsule. Ginger is successful since it trims down sugar longings and lessens inflammation in the system. It is imperative that one understands that if a person is to drop some pounds, things like get rid of inflammation, maintaining a healthy digestive system and intake of nutrients must be taken into account too.

There are many ways in which you could use the aforementioned essential oils for weight loss. Here are some ways which would benefit you in your journey towards weight loss.

- ✓ Aromatherapy
- ✓ Massages
- ✓ Usage of a diffuser
- ✓ Inhalation

CHAPTER 3: Recipes & Remedies with Essential Oils

1. Beauty and Well Being

For Face:

4 tablespoons Shea butter

2 teaspoons Vitamin E oil

10 drops Roman chamomile oil

2 drops Rose absolute oil.

Beat well till incorporated.

Anti-aging face mask

2 drops lavender essential oil

2 drops frankincense essential oil

1 teaspoon lemon juice

1/2 teaspoon plain, unflavored gelatin

2 teaspoons raw honey

1 egg yolk

Directions

1. In a bowl, whisk together all the ingredients until they are well combined.

2. Place a towel over your chest and shoulder area.
3. Wash your face as you normally do and then cover it well with the mask while it is still wet.
4. Let the mask dry completely. It should be tight on your face.
5. Wash it off by patting your skin with a warm, wet towel.
6. Repeat this process 1-2 times a week. The mask should be enough for 2 uses. Store the remainder in the refrigerator in a small jar. When you want to use it, allow it to come to room temperature first.

For Body:

2 tablespoons coconut oil,

1 teaspoon olive oil

1 teaspoon Vitamin E oil

2 drops tea tree oil

3 drops lime oil.

Beat well till incorporated.

After Sunburn:

1 cup distilled water (you can replace with part rose water)

3 tablespoons Aloe Vera gel

15 drops lavender oil

10 drops peppermint oil

Mix. Pour into spray bottle & spray onto sun burnt areas.

Bloodshot Eyes:

1 teaspoon olive oil

1 drop basil oil

2 drops lavender oil

A cold compress

Mix then apply to the region around your eyes (not past the socket bone). Never use on eyelids or eyes.

Broken Capillaries:

3 drops Roman chamomile oil

2 teaspoons Vitamin E

Rub onto broken capillaries two times a day to decrease the appearance and repair.

Citrus homemade deodrant

15-20 drops lemon essential oil

1/4 cuo arrowroot powder

1/4 cup baking soda

6 teaspoons coconut oil, melted

Directions

1. In a bowl, use a fork to mix together the arrowroot powder and baking soda.
2. Add the coconut oil and mash it in until you have a nice paste.
3. Add the essential oil and stir and then scoop the mixture into a jar.
4. Use the deodorant as needed.

Deodorant:

3 tablespoons coconut oil (solid)

2 tablespoons corn flour

2 tablespoons baking soda

8 drops tea tree oil

5 drops lime oil

4 drops grapefruit oil

(Include Vitamin E if you have sensitive underarms.)

Store in a glass jar and massage onto armpits, under breasts, lower back, thighs and other areas.

Easy homemade shower gel

2 teaspoons vegetable glycerin

5 drops Idaho Blue Spruce essential oil

10 drops ylang ylang essential oil

1 teaspoon jojoba oil

1 teaspoon vitamin E oil

2 tablespoons raw honey

2/3 cup Castile soap

Directions

1. Thoroughly whisk together the ingredients until they are well combined.
2. Pour the mixture in an 8-oz mason jar and close it with a soap pump lid for easy use.
3. Enjoy the shower gel whenever you take a shower.

Fungal Nail:

1 teaspoon coconut oil or olive oil

3 drops peppermint oil

Massage onto cleaned nails thrice a day. After the infection starts to diminish, continue treatment for 3 more days to guarantee it is gone for good.

Greasy Scalp Remedy:

Add 20 total drops of any blend of these oils to ½ cup of the conditioner and or shampoo:

Lemon

Cypress

Cedarwood

Lemongrass

Lavender

Peppermint

Ylang - ylang

Greasy Skin Remedy:

2 teaspoons salt

2-3 drops tea tree oil

2 teaspoons lemon juice

1 teaspoon honey

Blend together and massage onto oily skin and leave for 3-5 minutes. Wash with lukewarm water, then wet skin with icy water.

Holiday Body Butter

Essential oils of your choice

1/4 cup grapeseed oil

1/2 cup coconut oil (preferably extra virgin)

1-3/4 cups Shea butter (preferably unrefined)

Directions

1. Measure out the coconut oil and Shea butter and melt in a double broiler over medium-low heat. Stir the mixture constantly until you achieve a smooth consistency.

2. Allow the mixture to cool for 30 minutes and then add your favorite essential oil(s) and the grapeseed oil and stir.

3. Cover the mixture well and proceed to freeze for 20-30 minutes. Alternatively, you can refrigerate for about 1-2 hours. The mixture should solidify but it should not harden completely.

4. Place the mixture in a bowl and whip it until it is soft and fluffy. Spoon the body butter into a clean glass jar and use on your skin to add extra moisture anytime you need it.

Note: This butter is oily and it gets absorbed into your skin slowly. However, you can make it less oily by adding 1 ½ teaspoons of tapioca starch or arrowroot starch or cornstarch.

Homemade lavender lemon lip balm

Serves: 10-12 lip balm or chapsticks

Ingredients

Lip balm tins or chapsticks containers

2 drops vitamin E

7 drops lemon essential oil

7 drops lavender essential oil

4 tablespoons coconut oil

2 tablespoons bees wax

Directions

1. Melt the beeswax, vitamin E and coconut oil in a small pot over medium-low heat. Stir from time to time.
2. Remove the mixture from the heat and then add the essential oils throughout the mixture.
3. Pour the mixture quickly into the jars or tins and allow it to cool and harden.
4. Use as needed.

Make Up Cleaner:

2 drops of lavender oil

4 tablespoons vodka

2 tablespoons purified water

Pour all into a spray bottle. Spray onto tools and let to dry. You can also steep brushes, mascara wands, and pencils in this solution.

Make Up Remover:

2 drops tea tree oil

2 tablespoons olive oil

Apply solution with a cotton ball to tenderly remove make up.

Shaving Balm:

2 tablespoons coconut oil

2 drops tea tree oil

2 drops lemon oil

Beat the ingredients. Use as usual. (For body or non-acne prone skin only)

Skin care: (to be added to 100ml or 3.5oz carrier oil

Broken capillaries: 6 drops of cypress

6 drops of chamomile

8 drops of rose

Devitalised skin: 4 drops cypress

6 drops rose

10 drops geranium

Acne: 5 drops lavender

10 drops cypress

10 drops lemon

Mature skin: 6 drops ylang-ylang

6 drops frankincense

8 drops neroli

Dehydrated: 2 drops patchoulli

8 drops sandalwood

10 drops rose

Sensitive skin: 2 drops neroli

4 drops rose

6 drops chamomile

Dry skin: 6 drops rose

6 drops geranium

8 drops sandalwood

Oily**:** 6 drops lavender

8 drops lemon

8 drops sandalwood

Normal skin: 4 drops ylang-ylang

6 drops geranium

10 drops lavender

Super Glossy Hair:

3 drops peppermint oil

2 drops rosemary oil

250ml purified water.

Spray onto damp hair to add shine.

Toner:

1-2 drops rose absolute oil

1 cup jasmine green tea.

Use the tea bag as an applicator on skin. Lasts up to 2 days.

Toothpaste:

1 drop tea tree oil

1 drop peppermint oil

½ tablespoon coconut oil

1 teaspoon baking soda

Mix well and use as normal.

Tooth Whitening and Bad Breath Killer:

Peppermint oil

4% hydrogen peroxide

Coconut oil

Swish in mouth for 2 minutes 3 times daily. Continue for at least 8 weeks.

Whipped coconut oil moisturizer

Essential oil(s) of your choosing

20 drops lemon essential oil

20 drops lime essential oil

2 tablespoons aloe vera gel

1 tablespoon olive oil (or Castor oil)

1/2 cup coconut oil

Directions

1. Place all the ingredients into the mixing bowl. Refrain from melting the coconut first.
2. Use an electric mixer to whip the ingredients for 3-7 minutes or until the mixture has a light and airy consistency.
3. Place the whipped coconut oil moisturizer into a glass jar and ensure it is covered tightly. Store in the refrigerator or at room temperature to avoid melting the oil.
4. Use as desired.

Spider vein massage oil

2 oz. glass lotion pump bottle

1/4 cup grapeseed oil

8 drops helichrysum essential oil

10 drops cypress essential oil

Directions

1. Place the ingredients into the bottle and tightly place the cap on.
2. Gently shake the bottle to allow the ingredients to blend together and then allow the contents to marinate overnight.
3. When you want to use, you can squirt a few pumps into your hands and rub your palms together before massaging the oil into your legs in a gentle upward motion.
4. Massage 1-2 times a day as desired.

2. Home and Lifestyle

Bug repellent spray:

2 drops lavender oil

1 drop eucalyptus oil

250ml water

Mist onto skin via a spray diffuser.

Cleaning spray:

10-15 drops Citrus Fresh essential oil (per cup of cleaning spray)

1 part water

1 part distilled white vinegar

Dark glass spray bottle

Carefully pour water and vinegar into the dark spray bottle. Add 10-15 drops of essential oil and use for cleaning. Do not use vinegar on granite counter tops.

Flea Killer, suitable for pets:

1 cup apple cider vinegar

4 cups water

3 drops lavender oil

1 teaspoon lemon juice

Pour into a spray bottle and shake well. Spray on your pet twice every day, evading face and eyes. Spray onto their bedding too. Use this mix twice a week to prevent flea infections

Mirror polish:

Few drops of lemon essential oil

A duster.

Wipe mirrors to make them shiny and spotless.

Sleep aid:

Put any blend of the following oils into a diffuser, or add a few drops onto a unscented candle jasmine,

Lavender

Roman chamomile

Ylang-ylang

Sleep tight diffuser

1 drop ylang ylang

1 drop of patchouli

1 drop sweet marjoram

2 drops lavender

In a cold air diffuser, mix the oils with 70-100ml of water and diffuse as necessary.

Homemade sleep cream

8 oz. amber glass jar

Hand mixer

Double boiler

10 drops roman chamomile

10 drops cedarwood

15 drops rose

20 drops lavender

1/2 cup coconut oil

1 cup Shea butter

Directions

1. Melt the coconut oil and the Shea butter in your double boiler.
2. Remove the mixture from the heat and let it cool for a few minutes and then add the essential oils.
3. Stir to mix up the essential oils and then refrigerate the mixture for 15 minutes to allow it to partially solidify.
4. Remove from the refrigerator and use a hand mixer to whip it until it is a thick white cream.
5. Place the cream into an amber glass jar and store it in a cool dry place.
6. Rub the cream all over your body after you've had your shower or nighttime bath. You can use the cream on kids as well.

Calming diffuser blend: 1

2 drops sandalwood essential oil

2 drops lime essential oil

2 drops bergamot essential oil

2 drops grapefruit essential oil

Calming diffuser blend: 2

2 drops frankincense essential oil

1 drop Rosemary essential oil

2 drops orange essential oil

2 drops cedarwood essential oil

Stress and anxiety relief:

To a ratio of 1:1 salt and baking soda

Add one or a blend of the following oils:

Basil

Rosemary

Lemon

Peppermint

Lavender

Grapefruit

Surface cleanser:

5 drops grapefruit oil

5 drops lemon oil

100 ml strong vodka or rubbing alcohol

20-50ml purified water

Spray on counters, chopping boards, clothes, sofas and other surfaces to sanitize and purify.

Wood polish:

8 drops of lemon oil

4 tablespoons of olive oil.

Polish gently into wood to clean, and reinstate shine.

Odor eliminator diffuser

1 drop lime essential oil

1 drop cilantro essential oil

1 drop melaleuca essential oil

2 drops lemon essential oil

Immune booster essential oil diffuser

1 drop wild orange essential oil

1 drop clove essential oil

1 drop eucalyptus essential oil

1 drop rosemary essential oil

1 drop of cinnamon bark essential oil

Kitchen cleaning: oven

2 teaspoons liquid Castile soap

1/4 white vinegar

1 cup baking soda

1/2 cup salt

10 drops lemon essential oil

Directions

1. Preheat your oven to 309 degrees and then turn it off.
2. Mix together 1/2 cup water and 10 drops of lemon essential oil. Shake well and then carefully spray the mixture on the oven.
3. Mix together 1/4 cup of baking soda and 1/4 cup of salt and sprinkle on all the heavy spots.
4. Mix the remaining 3/4 cup of baking soda, 1/4 cup salt and 2 teaspoons Castile soap. The mixture should resemble a paste. Spread the paste on the entire interior of the oven and allow it to sit overnight.
5. In the morning, mix together 1/4 cup vinegar and 1/2 cup water and place the mixture into a spray bottle. Spray the mixture over the entire oven to allow the paste to loosen.
6. Proceed to wipe down and scrub the oven with a good amount of elbow grease
7. Wipe clean.

Kitchen cleaning: sink

1 oz. witch hazel

5 drops lemon essential oil

1/4 cup vinegar

Directions

1. In a glass spray bottle, mix together the hazel, lemon essential oil and vinegar.
2. Spray the mixture generously in and around your sink area.
3. Sprinkle the sink with some baking soda and then add a bit of elbow grease and scrub thoroughly.
4. Rinse clean.

Disinfectant

5 drops melaleuca (or tea tree) essential oil

2 drops wild orange

5 drops lavender

4 oz. bottle of distilled water

Shake the contents well and use to disinfect your hands, doorknobs, counters, toilet seats and other areas.

Toilet cleaner

10 drop eucalyptus or peppermint essential oil

1 tablespoon tea tree essential oil

1/4 cup liquid Castile soap

2 cups water

In a spray bottle, mix together all the ingredients and then shake well before use. You can spray the mixture on the toilet surface and then use a sponge or damp cloth to wipe clean.

Peppermint foam carpet shampoo

10 drops peppermint essential oil

3/4 cup liquid Castile soap

3 cups water

Directions

1. In a blender, combine all the ingredients.
2. Use a damp sponge to rub the foam into soiled areas.
3. Let the foam dry thoroughly before vacuuming.

3. Pain

Cooling body spray:

8 drops peppermint oil

Purified water

Spray on points where veins are visible.

Essential oils for arthritis: 1

2 drops geranium essential oil

2 drops lemongrass essential oil

2 drops wintergreen essential oil

2 drops cypress essential oil

2 drops frankincense essential oil

2 drops peppermint essential oil

Dilute the essential oils in a carrier oil and then apply 2-3 times a day on the affected area.

Essential oils for arthritis: 2

8 drops lavender essential oil

4 drops lemon essential oil

4 drops juniper berry essential oil

5 drops black pepper essential oil

In a small glass bottle, mix together 1 ounce of carrier oil and the essential oils. Massage the mixture on the affected areas several times per day.

Joint ache and rheumatism rub:

10 drops chamomile oil,

2 black pepper oil.

Massage into aching region.

Homemade heat balm

5 drops clove essential oil

7 drops eucalyptus essential oil

1 oz. beeswax

1/4 cup of olive, coconut or almond oil

9 drops peppermint essential oil

10 drops camphor essential oil

Directions

1. In a double boiler, mix together the oil and the beeswax until all the beeswax has melted. Make sure to stir well to combine the ingredients.

2. Place the mixture in a small glass jar or metal cosmetic tub and add in all the essential oils. Stir the ingredients gently but thoroughly.
3. Close the lid and allow the balm to cool in the container. You can use it after at least 2 hours.
4. Massage into sore joints and muscles for immediate relief.

Frankincense pain lotion

2 tablespoons vitamin E oil

1/4 cup coconut oil

1/4 cup olive oil

1/4 cup beeswax

1/4 cup shea butter

20 drops myrrh essential oil

20 drops frankincense essential oil

Directions

1. In a double boiler, mix together the shea butter, beeswax, coconut oil and olive oil and stir occasionally until the ingredients melt.
2. Place the mixture in the refrigerator for about 1 hour to allow it to solidify.
3. Remove from the refrigerator and beat with an electric mixer until fluffy.
4. Add the vitamin E and the essential oils and stir to combine.

5. Place the mixture in a cosmetic tub or glass jar and store.

6. You can use it anywhere on your body to relieve pain and stiffness.

Headache rub 1:

8 drops lavender oil

4 drops roman chamomile oil

OR 4 drops spearmint oil

8 drops lavender oil

Massage into forehead and temples ahead of sleep.

Headache rub 2:

4 drops peppermint oil

4 drops eucalyptus oil

Massage into temples and upper body

Soothing headache salve

Empty glass/metal container (with a lid)

10 drops of eucalyptus essential oil

10 drops of lavender essential oil

10 drops of peppermint essential oil

1/4 cup virgin coconut oil

Directions

1. Put hot tap water into a pan.
2. In a small bowl, add 1/4 cup coconut oil. Place the bowl in the pan to allow the heat to melt the oil.
3. Remove and add the essential oils and stir to combine. Pour the mixture into the glass/metal container.
4. Let the salve cool to room temperature and then refrigerate for one hour before use.
5. Use the salve on your forehead and temples. This will relieve tension headaches. You may want to store the salve in your fridge to avoid the coconut oil from liquefying.

Sore muscle balm

2 drops essential oils: lavender, black peppermint and ginger

5 drops of essential oils: eucalyptus, ginger, rosemary, camphor, peppermint, cinnamon

1 oz. beeswax

8 oz. sweet almond oil

Directions

1. In a double boiler, melt the almond oil and beeswax together.
2. Add the essential oils and stir to combine and then place the mixture into glass jars and close the lids.
3. Let the mixture cool to room temperature.

4. Massage the balm into sore muscles using circular motions. You can use the balm up to 3 times a day.

Period pain relief: 1

5 drops of peppermint oil

4 drops of lavender oil OR

4 drops of cinnamon oil

2 drops of nutmeg oil

4 drops of sweet orange oil

Gently massage into stomach and lower back

Period pain relief: 2

10 drops marjoram essential oil

12 drops Clary sage essential oil

20 drops lavender essential oil

2.5 ounces of your favorite carrier oil (you can use jojoba oil or an unscented massage lotion)

Directions

1. In a container or glass bottle, mix together all the ingredients and then massage the mixture gently into your lower back and abdomen area daily between periods.

2. Store the mixture in a cool dark place for later use.

Period pain relief: 3

2 ounces fractionated coconut oil or a carrier oil of your choice

2 drops cinnamon essential oil

4 drops geranium essential oil

5 drops ginger essential oil

7 drops fennel essential oil

6 drops marjoram essential oil

8 drops clary sage essential oil

Directions

1. In a roller bottle, mix together the essential oils and then add the fractionated coconut oil.
2. Shake the bottle well before each use.
3. Massage the menstrual relief tonic whenever you experience menstrual cramps.

Relaxing, joint pain rub:

4 drops cinnamon oil

3 drops sweet orange oil

Rub into joints

Muscle aches:

4 teaspoons plain base/carrier oil

2 drops rosemary oil

2 drops lavender

Mix together and use to massage your body gently.

4. Illness and Bodily Issues

Acid reflux/heartburn:

1 drop grapefruit oil (medical grade)

1teaspoon of baking soda

OR Andrew's salts

Mix into water and drink promptly.

Acne: 1

50:50 apple cider vinegar to water

Few drops of lavender/tea tree or basil oil.

Use a cotton ball to brush over affected areas. Twice a day daily would improve skin.

Acne: 2

1 drop frankincense essential oil

1 drop bergamot essential oil

1 drop ylang ylang complete essential oil

2 drops tea tree essential oil

1 drop carrot seed essential oil

2 drops lavender essential oil

Tamanu carrier oil

10ml roll-on bottle

Directions

1. Use the tamanu carrier oil to fill 2/3 of the roll-on bottle.
2. In the bottle, add the lavender, tea tree, ylang ylang, bergamot, carrot seed and frankincense essential oils in that order.
3. Shake the mixture well and then roll a small portion onto the blemishes.

Acne: 3

5 drops jasmine essential oil (optional)

5 drops lavender essential oil

5-10 drops vitamin E oil

10 drops frankincense essential oil

4 tablespoons unrefined jojoba oil

Mix all the ingredients together and pour the mixture into a dark bottle. Apply 4-5 drops of the mixture every morning and nighttime.

Allergy: 1

10 drops lemon essential oil

10 drops lavender essential oil

10 drops peppermint essential oil

In an amber dropper bottle, mix together all the oils. Diffuse 3-4 drops of the mixture or place a few drops on your handkerchief and breathe the mixture in every 1-2 hours.

Allergy: 2

10 drops peppermint essential oil

10 drops eucalyptus essential oil

10 drops basil essential oil

In an amber dropper bottle, mix the essential oils together and diffuse 3-4 drops of the mixture. You can also use a few drops on your handkerchief and breathe it in every 1-2 hours. If you wish to use the mixture on your skin, ensure you dilute to a 2% dilution before use.

Athletes foot spray:

10 drops peppermint oil,

7 drops lime oil with vodka

OR 2 per cent hydrogen peroxide.

Mist feet and the infection 2-3 times a day.

Cold and flu blend: daytime

6 drops Sweet orange (citrus sinensis)

5 drops Tea Tree (melaleuca alternifolia)

5 drops Eucalyptus (Eucalyptus globulus)

Cold and flu blend: nighttime

4 drops Sweet orange (citrus sinensis)

8 drops Frankincense (boswellia carterii)

6 drops lavender (lavandula angustifdia)

Constipation relief:

(Note: this is for mild constipation relief.)

1 drop ginger oil,

1 drop fennel oil

2 teaspoons of honey

Mix with hot water and drink warm.

Follow this with a methodical stomach massage of:

4 drops peppermint oil

3 drops black pepper oil

Massage clockwise with weight on the downward rub and light strokes upward.

Dandruff: 1

10 drops of lavender or tea tree oil

Coconut oil as needed

Rub into scalp, cover up with shower cap and leave overnight.
Treat once every week.

Dandruff: 2

4-6 ounces of water

2 drops lavender oil

2 drops lemongrass oil

2 drops oregano oil

Mix the essential oils and water together and stir before consuming as a tonic. The tonic is used internally to help maintain the proper PH balance of your scalp and this regulates sebum production.

Dandruff: 3

4 ounces of carrier oil (coconut oil or olive oil or almond oil)

1 teaspoon of raw honey

6 drops of tea tree oil

8 drops of cedarwood oil

8 drops of rosemary oil

Directions

1. Mix the oils together and stir well before pouring the mixture into a container.
2. Carefully apply the mixture on your scalp and proceed to massage gently for several minutes to allow the scalp to absorb the oil.
3. Let the scalp mask sit for at least 30 minutes and then rinse it off using some water and mild shampoo. You should use the scalp mask regularly until you find relief from dandruff.
4. You can let the mask sit overnight. Cover your hair using a shower cap if you do this.

Dandruff: 4

8 drops bay laurel or tea tree essential oil

8 drops lavender essential oil

1/2 cup apple cider vinegar (AVC)

1/2 cup distilled water

Directions

1. In a 4-oz container, mix together the bay laurel essential oil, lavender essential oil, vinegar and water and then shake well before you use the mixture.

2. Place a small amount of the anti-dandruff treatment into your palm and proceed to massage it into your scalp.

3. Allow it to sit for 5 minutes before rinsing it with water. Do not use shampoo. Use the treatment once a week.

4. Note: You may notice a strong smell for about an hour or so after using the treatment.

Eczema relief:

5 drops jasmine oil,

5 drops Roman chamomile oil

2 drops vitamin E oil

Shea butter/cocoa butter/liquid paraffin.

Liberally rub into distressed areas and leave overnight. Continue normal eczema treatment along with this

Head lice:

5 drops tea tree oil,

5 drops lavender oil

2 tablespoons of coconut oil

Rub into scalp and tips. Wear shower cap and leave on overnight.

Indigestion and gas:

7 drops of Roman chamomile oil

3 drops of cinnamon oil

2 tablespoons of coconut oil

Rub into abdomen.

Inflamed rash (lupus, psoriasis, allergy):

2 drops of lavender oil

1 teaspoon coconut oil (jojoba or olive on acne prone area)

½ teaspoon of vitamin e oil

Mix and rub onto inflammation after warm shower.

Nausea: abdomen massage blend

5 teaspoons carrier oil (macadamia, grapeseed, jojoba, sweet almond, sesame, coconut, argan)

3 drops peppermint

4 drops lavender

4 drops ginger

In a small nonreactive bowl, mix together the carrier oil and essential oil. Gently massage the blend on your solar plexus and abdomen area in a clockwise direction.

Nausea: Inhaler blend

Pocket sized inhaler for essential oils

3 drops geranium

5 drops spearmint

5 drops grapefruit

5 drops cardamom

5 drops bergamot

Mix together the essential oils in a non-reactive bowl. Put your inhaler wick into the bowl so that it can absorb the entire contents. Place the wick in the inhaler and ensure the cap is screwed back on tightly. Inhale the blend whenever necessary.

Sore throat: 1

1 drop Eucalyptus oil,

2 drop Cinnamon oil,

1 drop Lemon oil,

1 drop Clove oil in 1 fl oz. water

Or 50:50 mix of vodka and water.

Put in glass spray bottle and spray at back of throat.

Sore throat: 2

2 drops rosemary oil

2 drops eucalyptus oil

2 drops cinnamon oil

2 drops lemon oil

Sore throat: 3

2 drops frankincense

2 drops ginger

2 drops sweet orange

3 drops lemon

Toothache:

1 tablespoon of coconut oil

2 drops of peppermint oil,

1 drop of clove oil.

Swish gently in mouth for 10-20 minutes. Rinse with warm water and repeat.

Urinary tract infection:

¼ cup baking soda,

1 teaspoon vitamin c or citric acid,

1 drop lemon oil,

1 drop orange oil,

1 drop lime oil,

(Note: All oils must be medical grade to be consumed),

Non-sugar sweetener for taste

Simply mix ½ to 1 teaspoon with glass of water and drink every 3 hours relief.

Vaginal/anal/penile thrush:

3 cups of warm water

1 cup near boiling water with one of the following recipes:

3 drops rosemary oil

3 drops lavender oil

3 drops tea tree oil

OR 3 drops Lemongrass oil

2 drops clove oil

Immerse affected area in this solution.

Vaginal thrush treatment:

1 tablespoon of live yoghurt

3 drops of tea tree oil

Or lemongrass oil

Place into vagina using clean fingers or a tampon applicator.

Leave all night, rinse in the morning and replicate until infection is cleared.

Essential oils are extremely concentrated essences and should be taken care of with respect.

1. **Here are a few rules to guarantee safe usage of essential oils:**

- Use only 100% pure organic essential oils from plant life.

- Keep oils firmly closed and out of the reach of children.

- Never ingest undiluted oils. Use only oils meant for consumption.

- Do not apply undiluted oils on skin unless specified; always weaken with carrier oils.•

- Refrain oils from eyes and mucous membranes.

- If redness, burning, itching or irritation occurs, stop using oil right away.

2. **Steer clear of using any of the following oils during pregnancy:**

✓ Anise
✓ Bitter Almond
✓ Basil, Bay
✓ Birch
✓ Cedar Leaf
✓ Cedar Wood
✓ Citronella
✓ Clary Sage

- ✓ Clove Bud
- ✓ Geranium
- ✓ Hyssop
- ✓ Lavandin
- ✓ Spike Lavender
- ✓ Sweet Fennel
- ✓ Juniper berry
- ✓ Marjoram

- ✓ Myrrh
- ✓ Pennyroyal
- ✓ Peppermint
- ✓ Rose
- ✓ Rosemary
- ✓ Sage
- ✓ Thyme
- ✓ Wintergreen

3. These oils can be particularly irritating to the skin and should be experimented before use:

- ✓ Allspice
- ✓ Bay
- ✓ Bitter Almond
- ✓ Basil
- ✓ Birch
- ✓ Cajeput
- ✓ Cassia
- ✓ Cedar Leaf
- ✓ Cinnamon Leaf
- ✓ Clove Bud
- ✓ Sweet Fennel
- ✓ Fir Needle
- ✓ Lemon
- ✓ Lemongrass

- ✓ Peppermint
- ✓ Pine
- ✓ Tagetes
- ✓ Tea Tree
- ✓ Thyme
- ✓ Wintergreen

4. Epileptic people should refrain from using these oils:

- ✓ Cedar Leaf
- ✓ Hyssop
- ✓ Lavandin
- ✓ Sage
- ✓ Spike Lavender
- ✓ Sweet Fennel
- ✓ Rosemary

5. People with high blood pressure should keep away from:

- ✓ Hyssop
- ✓ Rosemary
- ✓ Sage
- ✓ Thyme
- ✓ Possibly toxic oils:
- ✓ Bitter almond (Prunus amygdalus var. amara),
- ✓ Inula (Inula graveolens),
- ✓ Khella (Ammi visnaga),
- ✓ Mugwort (Artemesia vulgaris),
- ✓ Pennyroyal (Mentha pelugium),
- ✓ Sassafras (Albidum),
- ✓ Thuja (Thuja occidentalis),
- ✓ Wintergreen (Gaultheria procumbens).

6. Very deadly essential oils: It is advised not use the following oils in any way.

- ✓ Ajowan (Ptychotis ajowan, Carum ajowan)
- ✓ Arnica (Arnica montana)
- ✓ Bolda (Peumus boldus)
- ✓ Bunch (Barosma betulina)
- ✓ Calamus (Acorus calamus)
- ✓ Cascarilla (Croton eluteria)
- ✓ Chervil (Anthriscus cerefolium)
- ✓ Deer tongue (Carphephorus odoratissimus)
- ✓ Horseradish (Cochlearia armoracia, Armoracia rusticana)
- ✓ Jaborandi (Pilocarpus jaborandi)
- ✓ Narcissus (Narcissus poeticus)
- ✓ Parsley (Petroselinum sativum, Carum sativum)
- ✓ Rue (Ruta graveolens)
- ✓ Santolina (Santolina chamaecyparissus)
- ✓ Spanish broom (Spartium junceum)
- ✓ Tansy (Tanacetum vulgare)
- ✓ Tonka (Dipteryx odorata)
- ✓ Wormseed (Chenopodium ambrosiodes, C. anthelmint
- ✓ Wormwood (Artemisia absinthium)

A Note of Thanks!

Thank you again for purchasing this book!

I hope this book was able to help you to identify essential oils that you can use for aromatherapy for the purpose of weight loss, health, and natural healing.

The next step is to go get your essential oils and use them for your natural health needs.

Finally, if you enjoyed this book, then I'd like to ask you a favor. Would you be kind enough to leave a review for this book on Amazon, please? I would greatly appreciate receiving your reviews!

I love getting feedback from my customers and reviews on Amazon. Your reviews really DO make a difference. If I get more good reviews, I will be able to publish more books. I read all my reviews and would really appreciate your thoughts.

Thank you and good luck!

ABOUT THE AUTHOR

Hello there! I am Brian James, your Canadian writer from Russia. Confusing already? I was born on the 24th of January 1990 in Moscow, to a Canadian couple who had immigrated to Russia. I was raised in Moscow till 2001, when I returned to my 'maple' roots. As Canadian as I am, I still feel fairly Russian too!

Academia was always a sore spot for me, since I was not all that fond of mathematics or science, and history was incredibly alien to me. The only things that interested me were sports and reading. Thanks to my mom, who taught me how to read as soon as I could make out the alphabet, I developed a voracious appetite for literature and simultaneously for fitness.

Along with these passions, I love food. I enjoyed learning about food and its effects on the human body. I yearned to combine fitness and food, so with great pleasure I enrolled in the University of Prince Edward Island in Charlottetown to pursue a degree in Food and Nutrition.

Today, I have joined my three obsessions together: food, fitness, and prose, to present to you my books, which detail everything you'll ever need to know about each topic.

Thank you for taking the time to peruse my work. May you have a wonderful, healthy life ahead of you. Good luck!

FREE BONUS REPORT

Lose The Weight For Good

WHICH DIET IS THE BEST FOR YOU?

There are so many diets out there that it's hard to decide which one is right for you. If you have tried one or several of these and didn't see the results you wanted or that they advertise, were you disappointed? Did you question yourself as to whether you could even lose weight? You might even be one of those people who say "I have tried every diet out there and just can't lose the weight"! Well maybe you have, though I highly doubt it because I can tell you there are A LOT, hundreds if not thousands of diets out there so I am sure you haven't tried every single one.

The thing you have to remember is that not every diet will work on everyone. We each have our own metabolism and how it works with us and our body will be the determining factor in whether a diet is going to work for you or not. Some of us have to lower our calorie intake, fewer carbs, less sugar or fat etc. Others have to eat many smaller meals throughout the day to keep our metabolism up so that we burn fat and calories.

It's not necessarily what you eat all the time but more HOW you eat. If you eat 3 big meals a day and then have a few snacks throughout the day and can't seem to lose weight well stop and think about what you are eating and why. There are so many factors when it comes to losing weight that you can't just find a fix all diet and think that "this time it will work" because nine times out of 10 it won't and you will feel even worse in the end and probably gain weight instead of losing. If you stop and think about it, how many of you have decided "I am never going to lose weight so I might as well just eat what I want and be happy; after all you only live once"?

It usually doesn't take much to push someone over the edge that has been on a roller coaster with dieting and just decides to give up. I know this doesn't sound too positive

but we will get to that later. I can honestly tell you that you CAN lose weight if you really want to, and it doesn't have as much to do about the food you eat but when, how, what and why you eat. It also has much to do with how active you are.
So let's stop thinking about food being the issue and start looking inside and see what we come up with. After all, if you have already tried 'every diet out there' what can it hurt to read a little and see if it doesn't click with you.

WHY WHAT YOU EAT IS IMPORTANT TO LOSING WEIGHT?

Let's start by taking a look at what you eat. What foods are you addicted to, what are your favorite foods? What foods can you not live without? We all have foods we say we can live without, wouldn't bother us if say brussel sprouts fell off the side of the earth not to be seen again. I use them as an example because I am the only one in my family that likes them, my husband and kids wouldn't mind if they never existed. I happen to love them, now I could live without them, but they aren't one of my favorite foods. I personally love cheese, love, love, love it! Could I LIVE without it? Probably, would I want to? No! Too many of my favorite foods include cheese and so I think it would be hard to live without those foods. Ok, in the literal sense yes, I am sure my body could survive, but I don't think I would be too happy in the end.

What about you? What foods would it be hard for you to let go? What foods do you crave? Now that you have those in mind I want you to write them down on a piece of paper. Now that you have them written down I want you to write WHEN you usually eat them. For instance, I crave certain foods now and again and in my mind I believe the reason I crave them is because my body is lacking in a certain vitamin or mineral and so when it comes to the healthier foods I will give myself permission to eat these foods i.e. broccoli, liver, corn etc. There are also those foods that I just crave because they are so yummy; chocolate cake, potato chips, ice cream…These are foods that I also allow myself now and then because I know that if I deny myself I won't be happy and I will eat just about anything trying to satisfy the craving, which would probably lead to ingesting more calories than if I had eaten that cookie in the first place!

What you need to understand is that the more you deny yourself what you want the more you are going to crave it and the more likely you are to abuse the craving in the end. You crave a cookie, have A cookie, or two, but don't have six or seven or ten or the whole bag! Be good to you and you will be a happier person in the end and you can still lose weight believe it or not! I know you are doubting what I am saying but keep reading and you will see where I am going. I am not a doctor or dietitian I don't have a degree nor am I a weight loss counselor. I am just like you, I have tried and failed many times and have found out a few things over the years that actually opened my eyes and to my surprise (or maybe not so much) I started losing weight!

WHY THE DIETS YOU TRY DON'T WORK?

When it comes to weight loss you can't just diet and lose a few pounds and think that's it, you're all done and good to go. Losing weight is a lifestyle choice and a total change in how you eat and what you do. Sure you can go on a diet and restrict yourself, there are thousands out there! I am sure you have heard of the grapefruit diet and cabbage soup diet but think about what that means. It means truly restricting yourself from all of the foods you really like and eating only what you are told to eat. You lose a bunch of weight and feel great (or maybe not so because you haven't been able to eat your favorites) and you quit the diet. You've lost the weight you wanted to so why continue?

Well now here you are 10, 15, 20 pounds lighter and looking better and feeling better, your clothes are fitting much better and maybe you even have to go buy new clothes! You are so excited for the new you and can't imagine a better feeling. The diet worked and you start telling all of your friends about it and they decide to try it and everyone is excited. The diet stops, the weight starts creeping back on and you wonder where you failed.

It failed because it didn't teach you the one most important thing when it comes to dieting. HOW to eat what you usually eat and keep the weight off!! Those pre-made packaged food diets do the same thing; they don't teach you how to portion your own meals correctly so once you get off of them you start putting the weight back on. So now what? Where do you go from here? If no diet will truly work what hope is there for losing weight?

You can and will lose weight as soon and you find your groove and stick to it! Yes you can still eat your favorite foods and lose weight, yes you can go to parties and enjoy and lose weight and yes you can go on vacations and lose weight. Isn't it great to be able to say YES to yourself? You need to be able to say no also though. No you don't need that extra helping, no you don't need an extra piece of cake and no you can't sit idle and expect to lose any weight. You need to know the limits and stick to them without having to deny yourself anything. If you can remember this one thing, I can ALMOST guarantee you that you will still lose weight even if you do nothing else.

It takes 20 minutes for your stomach to register full; in other words it takes about that long for the food to get into your stomach and the signal that there is food in there to reach your brain. If you can wait 20 minutes before you go and get seconds you will most likely realize you are not hungry and don't need that second helping. Surprised? Try it and see!

WHY YOU WILL FAIL IF YOU DIET?

When I talk about not denying yourself the foods you love I am not saying to go all out and eat as much as you want. I once watched a show where they had a lady who was celebrating her 104th birthday and the interviewer asked her how she was able to live for so long (she was smoking a cigarette!) and she said “Everything in moderation”. The interviewer went on to ask her if she watched what she ate, if she drank alcohol etc. and she said yes, she did all that but never to excess.

So I suppose that is what I am telling you, eat what you like but never to excess. You also need to look at your health, if there is a medical reason for you to avoid certain foods then do so. It’s not all about losing weight it’s also about making sure you are physically healthy. I was told I had high cholesterol, well my triglycerides were high but my hdl and ldl were fine. There is a lot of technical language they use on how they figure this, but all I needed to know is that I had to change my diet to get it lowered or they would have to put me on medication. So it was changed and it worked! Boiled, broiled, grilled and baked foods, avoid fried foods and of course the fewer processed foods, the better.

Yes, I do still have some fried food now and then but not nearly what I use to, I use butter on rare occasions, and yes I still have dessert when I want to. I know I could not live happily if I were to deny myself some of my favorite foods all the time, but I also know I want to be around for a very long time, hopefully to see my grandkids graduate one day!

So if you think about the last 2 things I have told you and you combine them do you think you could lose weight? I am guessing the answer is yes. You can’t move forward if you remain still, you can't lose weight if you continue eating the way you are and not moving or changing anything. It's like the old joke about the guy who prays daily to win the lottery and never wins and God tells him he can't win if he doesn't buy a ticket. Hoping, wishing and praying won't help you lose weight, you have to DO something, make a change in your life in order to move forward.

If you drink soda, stop. Just that one thing will help you lose some weight, you might not lose it real quick and you might not see it right away but it will work! Imagine all the little calories you consume during the day. Look at the label on your soda, how many servings is it, and how many calories per serving...that can add up very quickly! So do yourself a favor and try to quit drinking soda if at all possible or check the label of whatever it is you do drink on a daily basis.

DIFFERENCE BETWEEN MEN AND WOMEN FOR LOSING WEIGHT

I always laugh when I watch that commercial where the wife says she stopped drinking soda and lost 1 dress size and her husband lost 3 or however it goes. I laugh because it's true! I have seen it with my own eyes. My husband was diagnosed with diabetes about 4 years ago; it was brought on by a very stressful situation and got pretty bad. He hates taking pills of any kind so was determined to change his diet to control his diabetes. We were not together at that time, well we were married but I was with his parents because his father was ill and had our oldest daughter with me, he was back home 12 hours away with our other 2 children (they were still in school) and trying to work our home business, take care of the kids and the house and trying to sell our house.

Yes stress can trigger more than ulcers and heart attacks! The kids said he was doing great, had started eating a salad every day stopped drinking soda and started exercising. Within a few months he had lost quite a bit of weight and was actually able to stop his medication (do NOT do this without your doctors approval!) and was feeling much better; that same few months I had been crazy busy cleaning, painting running around and keeping busy at his parents. I wasn't eating as much but just wasn't dropping the weight the way he had been able to and I didn't understand why.

As his changes kept his weight loss on track mine was just stuck and I started getting depressed. I just didn't know what I could do to get the weight to fall off as I was more active than I had been in a long time and yet it was real slow going.

Men and women lose weight differently and women have to take into account their age and hormone balance also! I had, had a hysterectomy years before; 11 to be exact and at that time I was in pretty good shape. I probably could have lost a few pounds but nothing

I was concerned about. It seemed that every year that passed I gained more weight and it was harder and harder for me to take it off. 3 years ago I started hormone treatments and to my surprise the weight started falling off much more easily than it ever had. Hormones for women are very important when it comes to weight loss, if the balance is off it can mean the difference between losing 1 pound or 10. I haven't lost all the weight I want to yet but it keeps coming off so I am happy about that! A few more changes and I am sure I can have it right where I want it to be, but it's up to me and nobody else to make those changes if I want to lose the rest of the weight.

GETTING IN YOUR GROOVE AND STICKING WITH IT

When it comes to losing weight it's important for you to get into your groove. You need to lose weight for you and only you; because your parents, friends, significant other are getting on you about your weight is not reason enough to lose it and in most cases will cause the opposite effect. So when you set out to lose the weight; do it because it is what you want and not what others want you to do so you are not setting yourself up for failure.

Find at least 1 activity you really enjoy doing and do it with all you have! If you like bike riding then get a good bike and go out and ride. Even if you are only going around the block at first don't give up, after awhile you will be able to do that block a few times without effort and pretty soon you will find yourself going a mile or two or more! The point is to get you up and moving, doing something you don't do on a daily basis because that is something you aren't used to doing and you will start losing weight because you are adding an element into your lifestyle that you hadn't had before.

For me it was Badminton and I know how silly that might sound to some but for me it has worked wonderfully! Actually I hadn't played much and then a couple of years ago we decided to get a net and racquets for a family gathering and we played daily for weeks! We even tried finding glow in the dark birdies but no go. I had decided to weigh myself after the first 3 days of playing just to see and I had lost 6#'s! I know that sounds impossible but I seriously had which kept me playing and at time begging my kids or hubby to come out for awhile and now we are all hooked!

So yes, find something you enjoy and take advantage of it, you will have fun and lose weight at the same time. Anything you do, any change you make in your normal routine when it comes to fitness will have some impact on not only your health but your weight. Let's say you walk around the house quite a bit, a little up and down stairs cleaning or picking up after yourself or the kids and with your daily routine you have been stuck at the same weight for months or even years. When you ADD something else to your routine you are getting more of a workout, you're changing things up and burning more calories than you had been.

I am sure you can see the benefits of this and why you could lose weight making even one change in your everyday routine. It doesn't have to be difficult really it doesn't and you don't have to starve yourself or go on some odd diet. Those are for people who want or need to drop weight quickly for an event or party and are not looking at a long term weight loss goal.

THAT DREADFUL TIME OF DAY

Weight loss is more than just watching what you are eating, it's about your whole lifestyle, the way you live day to day not just eating salads or starving yourself (which by the way is the worst way to lose weight!) or spending a ton of money on gimmick diets that won't work long term. When you think about losing weight why wouldn't you want the weight loss to stick? Why do something you know you can't stick with which would only cause you to gain the weight back again and then you have to start all over?

We all have a time of day when we get tired and just want to take a little nap, admit it its true! Mine is around 4pm and usually I would lay down and just give in to that feeling and take a little nap but I found that on days that I just couldn't do that usually within about 20 minutes I would be awake and alert again and felt good. So I have pushed myself through that time of day over and over again and now I no longer take that midday nap and I actually feel better about not having taken a nap!

These are the little things you really need to think about and the changes you can make in your daily routine that will make all the difference when it comes to losing weight. When you feel that nagging to go lay down and take a little nap get up and move. Go take a walk or a short bike ride or work in the yard; anything other than giving in to laying down for a bit and after a couple of weeks you won't need that afternoon snooze anymore.

So now we have talked about 3 or 4 different changes you can make to your lifestyle that will help in your weight loss goals and these are just very small changes, imagine what you could accomplish if you made even bigger changes; Changes that would really kick up your weight loss into high gear and lose even faster. Things like skipping a daily dessert or a snack or eating leaner meat and more veggies. Trading a fattier snack for a healthier snack; say carrot and celery sticks with ranch instead of potato chips.

If you start out making small changes in your diet and lifestyle it won't be as hard as making a bunch of big changes all at once and you probably won't even notice some of them after a short time and will wonder why you even did it in the first place. I use to drink diet Pepsi all the time, but then started having issues with kidney stones so gave it up, it took me a week to get it out of my system and I got over the headaches in a few days but looking back I wonder why I drank it at all.

Do something for yourself that you know will last, that you can be proud of and when you look in the mirror or step on the scale you can smile knowing that you aren't going fall back into old habits because you have made new ones!

GIVING YOURSELF PERMISSION TO CHEAT NOW AND AGAIN

We all have days when we just don't want to; don't want to NOT eat that cupcake, don't want to take a walk, don't want to skip that nap and don't want to eat the fish instead of the burger. It's OK! Give yourself permission to give in now and again. This isn't to say it should be a once a week thing, but if you have had a particularly hard day or week give yourself a freebie. It is ok to treat yourself now and then and not feel guilty but don't make a habit of it, don't do it too frequently that you forget why you weren't doing it in the first place.

For instance, if you know you will be having a busy weekend out and about with friends or family and you won't be watching what you eat or how much or might be over indulging then give yourself that gift. You have worked hard so far so why shouldn't you enjoy yourself. Just make sure it isn't often enough to sabotage your new lifestyle!

If you stop and think about seasons you can see a pattern of over eating possibilities. Summer, you have BBQ's, Graduation Parties and of course the 4th of July, Fall and Winter bring Thanksgiving, Christmas and New Years and throughout the year there will be Birthdays and Anniversaries so spread things out, think before you decide to which parties you want to go to and just be a little more careful with how and what you eat that month. Maybe pick up on the movement, walking or bike riding a little more anything to keep the momentum up and not falling back on your promise to yourself.

It is difficult I know, been there! There are times when you think you are going to gain a few pounds but remember muscle weighs more than fat, if you are working out more and your clothes are not getting tighter (the best indicator of weight gain) don't worry about what the scale says. You might also not want to weigh yourself too often, usually once a week at most or even less, once every two weeks will be just fine. You weight is always fluctuating on a daily basis so weighing yourself every day will do nothing but depress you.

You can actually gain a few pounds during the day from bloating and water, another reason not to weigh yourself daily. Give yourself at least a week before you weigh yourself and do it in the morning before you eat. Write those numbers down in a journal and keep track, you will see how much your weight fluctuates on a monthly basis. You might also want to start a food journal keeping track of what you eat and how it effects your weight, this of course is completely up to you, I never kept one but keep mental notes on what I have eaten during the day and how I feel that night (bloated, full, heavy etc.). Whatever works for you!

WHY WHAT YOU DRINK CAN SABATOGE YOUR DIET?

You wouldn't think that what you drink throughout the day would affect your weight all that much but if you take a real close look you will see that it can and does! Do this little experiment and you will see what I am talking about; don't drink anything but water for one whole day, that's right only water, you can add fresh lemon or lime if you want but nothing else. Do you think you're eating habits would change by drinking only water? Do you think you would eat more or less or differently? I think you will be surprised.

There are studies out there and if you watch a certain Dr. show you will know that people that tend to lean towards sweet drinks such as soda tend to eat or snack more during the day. The reason for this is that you end up craving something salty to wash down the sweetness of the drink. Also if you look at a normal can of soda there are 150 calories PER CAN! If you drink nothing but soda all day long you will have used up close to or over half of the 2500 calorie daily allowance!

Does that surprise you? Just think of how many calories you can save just by changing this one bad habit! Not everyone drinks enough water anyway and most of the time when you are feeling down and tired and like you are dragging it's because you are dehydrated. Caffeine in colas and coffee and energy drinks actually dehydrate your body. Not to mention, most energy drinks are 2-3 servings per can or bottle so drinking 1-3 a day...think about the calories you are consuming!

Now we are going to talk about alcohol...yes it does have calories and the sweeter the drink the more calories, beer alone has plenty, mixed drinks even more. I personally am not a drinker but do have one now and again, but there are those that drink their wine daily or at least with dinner, and while red wine does have its benefits, and I hear even beer can help with kidney stones, everything in moderation is the best way to think. You have seen plenty of people with “beer bellies” so just keep that in mind when you are at a party and getting your drink on. Not to mention the after effects, I don’t know of anyone who enjoys a hangover.

I think you will notice when you try this water experiment you will find you feel fuller faster, you won’t be as tired or edgy or feel like you are dragging through the day, you will eat less or snack less and will feel all over much better for it! Sticking to it might be hard, but if you can it will do you a world of good! I am NOT a water drinker at all! But I have found a recipe for infused water that I find delicious, look up infused water online and I think you too will enjoy it, especially on a hot summer’s day!

WHEN YOU CAN LOOK IN THE MIRROR AND SMILE YOU HAVE MADE IT!

Once you start making these little changes you will start to notice a change in your mood, energy level, eating habits and most of all in the overall way you feel about yourself. You might have to start buying new clothes because the ones you have are just too loose and that alone will give you a huge confidence boost! They are small changes but they work, I know this because they have worked for me when nothing else would, or I couldn't imagine eating only 3 items for a week to lose 10 pounds knowing I would just go back and eat what I want in the end.

For women over 40, go to your family doctor and tell them you want your hormone levels checked, if they are off, this alone can be one reason you are having trouble losing weight. I had a very hard time, no matter what I did and once they got my levels to where they should be I felt incredible and the weight started dropping pretty fast. I can't imagine my life without the balance in my hormones and yes it can be expensive, but for me and my family (they will not let me stop!) it's something that is worth it. I was constantly tired, moody, weight gain, irritable etc. Now with my levels where they should be I can't even remember how bad I was before...oh but my family can! ;)

Just remember these are all small changes you can make in your daily routine, changes that will become good habits and the end result will be a happier, healthier and thinner you!! You also want to remember that this is something you are doing for yourself, not because others think you should. You don't want to be pushed into something that will make you resentful and actually sabotage what you are trying to accomplish but for you to start something you KNOW you CAN do and keep up with so that you don't fail, because you won't fail it's too easy!

Here are some supplements that might help you all around and keep you moving forward with the happy new you: B12 complex, Vit D, VitC, DHEA (hormone balancing supplement). Taken together they will help with energy and mood and if you are like me, when you don't have energy you can GET the energy you need to DO anything, it's a vicious cycle and it kills everything including your self-esteem and confidence. I hated being tired all the time because I just didn't have the energy to do anything I knew I should do let alone what I wanted to get done. Before you start any program or take any supplements make sure you talk with your family Dr. and that you are able to take them without any ill effects.

As I said in the beginning I am not a professional, I just know what has worked for me when nothing else did and I hope that my tips and tricks help you too!

30063606R00063

Printed in Great Britain
by Amazon